Shining Through The Process of *Purpose*

Chara A. Taylor

Love Clones Publishing
www.lcpublishing.net

Copyright © 2015 by Chara A. Taylor. All rights reserved. This book or any portion thereof may not be reproduced or used in any manner whatsoever without the express written permission of the publisher except for the use of brief quotations in a book review.

Printed in the United States of America

First Printing, 2015

ISBN: 978-0-692-40963-3

King James Version Scripture quotations marked "KJV" are taken from the Holy Bible, King James Version (Public Domain).

New King James Version
Scripture quotations marked "NKJV" are taken from the New King James Version. Copyright © 1982 by Thomas Nelson, Inc. Used by permission. All rights reserved.

Publishers:
Love Clones Publishing
Dallas, TX 75205
www.lcpublishing.net

Dedication

This book is joyfully dedicated to all Girls Entering Womanhood While Experiencing Life's Struggles. May you embrace the gifts and calling on your lives and may you shine through your process to your destined purpose so you can shine in His purpose for you.

You are a jewel, you are destined to shine!.

Thanks & Acknowledgments

I would like to begin by thanking the Lord God Almighty, creator of what is now and what is to come. Thank You LORD for orchestrating my life's path, always knowing what is best for me, and for keeping my mind stayed on You when I had to endure waiting seasons. I want to thank my Lord and Savior Jesus Christ for being all that I need when I am in need. Thank You for being Peace for me along the path to purpose. And a special thanks to the Holy Spirit for being my Guide along the way.

I would like to say "THANK YOU" to my ribcage, my husband, Bishop Ronald E. Taylor Jr., who has always believed in me, trusted me, supported me, encouraged me, and provided the funds to do what I need to do. Your faithfulness to God, me, our family, marriage, and ministry are evident in how you live and take care of us. You are truly a man after God's own heart and I honor and respect you as my earthly lord and king, as my covering.

I would like to thank my baby boy, Isaac Jeremiah Taylor. Your life inspires me to continue on in this journey to purpose knowing that what I do affects you. You are truly a reward from God and I love you more than I can comprehend.

I would like to acknowledge and thank my spiritual parents, Apostles Robbie and Sharon Peters. Apostles Robbie and Sharon Peters, you are answered prayer. Your love, leadership, and impartation has epically changed the course of my life both spiritually and naturally. I love you both and appreciate all you do for us as a family and for the kingdom.

I would like to thank ALL my sisters of Kingdom Empowerment International Covenant Fellowship of Churches, Inc. in St. Louis, MO and Chicago, IL. All of these strong Women of God have been a driving force for me. I am so grateful for each of you and your unyielding love, supportive conversations, powerful prayers, help with deliverance (Apostle Tonya Stewart) and words of encouragement. Love you my Sisters!

I would like to thank my mother and sisters (Deborah, Tavera, & Ann Cheree) for a great life that I would not change – I love you! I would like to give a special thanks to Pastors Willie and Cecilia Holloway, Pastor Prophetess Sharon E. Tyson, Elder Lisa King,

Deacon Jimmy Wilder, Uncle James and Aunt Roxy Perry, Aunt Geraldine Peeples, Joe and Marie Lieway, and Pastor Stacy Garner; I am forever indebted to you for all your wisdom, support, help, and belief in the vision of GEWWELS . I would like to thank Love Clones Publishing and Apostle Candace Ford for believing in me as an author and working so diligently with me to birth this and other pieces of work.

Table of Contents

Foreword..8

Preface...14

Introduction...22

Chapter 1 – Childhood...50

Chapter 2 – Family..68

Chapter 3 – Friends & Social Relationships..............80

Chapter 4 – Men & Relationships..............................90

Chapter 5 – Church Hurt...98

Chapter 6 – A New Beginning – Shining In God.....109

Foreword

Diamonds are associated with love and romance. It is the stone traditionally chosen for engagement rings. And, rightly so, because diamonds foster unity, trust, and fidelity.

When a diamond specialist examines a diamond, he looks at all of its facets and sides. Shimmering different colors from each angle, the diamond reveals something new about itself as it is manually rotated under the light. Mental prayer essentially does the same thing. It considers some aspect of Christ's life or spiritual truth by looking at it and studying it. It then submits the many aspects of our life as we know it - with all of its disappointments and promises – to the Light of Christ so that the good and the bad may be seen for what they really are.

Have you ever known an individual who on the surface seemed shy, modest, and ordinary, but behind it all was the most loving, gracious person you've ever met? They abound in exceptional talent and good works; yet, they are your typical unsung hero. They rise to the occasion in a time of need and shine best in trial's darkest hour and seasons of severe tests. Such a person is one whom we would call a diamond in the rough. Like naturally occurring diamonds, they appear quite ordinary, even rough on the outside, but their beauty and worth comes from the extreme pressure under which they are formed and the harsh process of cutting and polishing that are used to reveal their inner beauty and value.

Every one of us is a potential diamond in the rough. Embedded within each person are diamond-like qualities waiting to be mined bringing joy to our Maker, others, and ourselves. Are we willing to endure the pressure, the cutting, and the polishing of the Master Jeweler to bring out the diamond within us? Most of us are not.

Let's take a look at diamonds and see how their formation and qualities parallel the lives of true believers.

A diamond is just carbon (essentially the same thing as charcoal) in a very concentrated form. Yet, when mined, cut, and polished, it becomes the most precious gemstone in the world. As we try to imagine the extreme temperature and pressure under which diamonds are formed, it brings to mind the fiery trials which children of God must undergo to develop true godly character. 1 Peter 1:6-7 describes the beautiful outcome of being tested by God's fire:

"In this you greatly rejoice, though now for a little while, if need be, you have been grieved by various trials, that the genuineness of your faith, being much more precious than gold that perishes, though it is tested by fire, may be found to praise, honor, and glory at the revelation of Jesus Christ."

The conditions of high pressure and temperature way beneath the Earth's crust must be ideal for carbon to form into diamond. Slightly less than this, we end up with graphite (a soft black mineral) instead of the extremely hard, clear crystal we know as diamond. That's why we have to be willing to endure the pain of trials and godly discipline if we want God's character to be perfected in us.

"My brethren, count it all joy when you fall into various trials, knowing that the testing of your faith produces patience. But let patience have its perfect work, that you may be perfect and complete, lacking nothing" (James 1:2-4).

A diamond is the hardest known mineral. It's so hard that it can only be scratched by another diamond. It's the unique molecular structure of the carbon atoms that makes a diamond very hard. As we allow Christ to live in us we will have His diamond-hard strength to withstand the pressures of life and not be easily scratched or wounded by the words or deeds of others.

Before diamonds become beautiful jewels, they must be cut and polished by hand or machine using steel or diamond blades or laser. The cut diamond is then polished by a rotating wheel coated with an abrasive diamond powder. God's purpose is to refine and perfect us. He will use whatever means necessary to bring us to the point of being "a perfect man, to the measure of the stature of the fullness of Christ" (Ephesians 4:13).

Diamonds are judged according to the four C's:
1. Cut – the geometric shape into which it has been cut
2. Clarity – a measure of its flaws, or inclusions that can be seen in the diamond
3. Carat – the weight of the diamond (in milligrams)
4. Colour – ranging from icy white transparent to light yellow.

Here, too, we can see some similarities with the life of the believer.

Cut - The more we come under the sharp edge of God's Word and allow it to pierce and shape us, the more valuable we will be for His Kingdom. His desire is that our lives be transparent and flawless. We must be sincere and true (1 Corinthians 5:8).

Clarity - As the apostle Paul says, we must not have "spot or wrinkle or any such thing," but rather "be holy and without blemish" (Ephesians 5:27). Like flawless diamonds we must reflect and disperse light because we are the light of the world to disperse the darkness of this evil age (Matthew 5: 14-16).

Carat and Colour - God's diamonds will be judged, not by the colour or roughness of their exterior, but by the content and quality of their interior, in a word, by their character.

This character is developed, not inherited. It cannot be bought, it must be earned. It cannot be achieved by avoiding God's divine process. We must be willing to endure the Master Jeweler's refining process. It is this process that will shape and refine us from being diamonds in the rough to become sparkling jewels.

The most precious gems in the world cannot be compared to those who will shine like diamonds in the Heavenly Father's realm on that day when He makes up His jewels (Malachi 3:17).

This book is a brilliant masterpiece of you seeing yourself going through a process and I assure you that you will shine brightly.

Apostle Robbie C. Peters
Presiding Prelate and Chief Apostle
The Kingdom Empowerment International Covenant Fellowship of Churches, Inc.

Preface

Have you ever wondered why it seems that your life is always filled with turbulent life altering situations? Have you ever felt like you are the only person going through tough times? Finally, have you ever questioned why those who do not serve God appear to be succeeding in life and not you – even though you serve Him with every fiber of your being? I'm here to tell you that every obstacle you experience is designed to thrust you into the place and position where you can shine. That's right – you were created to shine but you can only shine in the place God has destined for you. You are a GEWWEL (Girl Entering Womanhood While Experiencing Life's Struggles and GEWWELS (Jewels) shine!

A diamond shines only when it goes through a long arduous process. Before the rough diamond is transformed into a beautiful piece of jewelry, it must undergo several stages in its production. After it goes from its original mining stage to its cutting stage, it finally reaches the point where it is ready to be polished and sold to fulfill its purpose. The same is true for GEWWELS. As females, we do not enter into womanhood without experiencing life obstacles or struggles. The process is what makes us! Let's continue with our study of the diamond. Many of us love diamonds, we will spend thousands of dollars to get the largest diamond, the one that looks the prettiest, the one that looks the best on our hand, the one people can see from miles away. It must be the correct cut, the correct weight, and must make jaws drop open when it is seen. I always said that I wanted my wedding ring to be seen from an airplane that's 30,000 feet in the clouds. We have our individual desires and thoughts on how we want our diamonds to look and what we will use each diamond for. Well, that is how God feels about us – we are His GEWWELS – individualized and destined to shine in His purpose.

Diamonds and jewelry in general, enhance our appearance. Earrings brighten our face; necklaces highlight our neckline, and bring out our outfits. Bracelets sparkle on our wrists and rings make our hands talk. Rings tell if we are married or single by what finger they adorn. When we wear jewelry we are making statements. The only way each piece can fulfill its purpose is to go through a jewelry making manufacturing process. Without the process, it cannot shine; it cannot fulfill its purpose. Without the process, expensive price tags cannot be applied to it to mark its value. Without the process people all over the world would not fight to get to it first. Without the complete process, there is no maximum purpose. If it only undergoes half the process it will only complete half its purpose. The same is true with us – God's GEWWELS; each of us were intrinsically created for a specific purpose here in the earth. We all share the same purpose, which is to love God, to reverence Him, commune with Him and obey Him. In addition, each of us will find ourselves wearing the same hats as other women but with different paths to get there.

For example, many of us will be daughters, sisters, wives, mothers, or friends. However, just because we have the same titles, does not mean our destinies are the same and neither is our route to get to these destinations. Each of us has our individual purposes, which will ultimately result in God's promises manifested in our lives as blessings, miracles, favor, and abundance. The key is not to fight the process! Jesus prayed to His Father, God let your will be done on earth as it is in heaven. It is meant for us to experience it here first in order to have a real appreciation and anticipation for it in heaven. We will learn later on in the book how to tell if what we are experiencing is part of God's divine will or His permissive will or a result of a choice we made without His approval. We will also see that the process will include some pain and some loss sometimes, but in the end it will result in joy, abundance, love, and life eternally.

What I find strikingly amazing about diamonds and jewelry is that although each one is different and made for a different person, they are not competing with one another. They are sitting beautifully side by side in the display case awaiting its purpose partner to arrive and put it into position. I can imagine they are pushing and encouraging each other saying, is it me, yet or is today your turn?

Each diamond or piece of jewelry sits waiting patiently to enhance its owner – they wait anticipating shining in purpose. They know they cannot shine to the max in the display case because they were designed to adorn bodies. They don't need to do any extra for attention or to be noticed, their value was determined before its position on the market. Its name tells its value. When we hear diamond we know its value. When people know we are children of God they will know our value. When we present ourselves as God's Daughter, we show our value. When we refuse to lower our standards we refuse to be devalued. When we refuse to accept mediocrity, we display our worth. We are of a royal lineage; we are a chosen generation and the price that was paid for our lives make us rare and expensive. We cannot be cheapened because of today's cultural standards. We only live in this world, we are not of this world and our worth is not determined according to the standards of America; our standards, our wealth, our prosperity and our success is determined according to the promises of God.

Diamonds are respected – people make sure to take care of them. They are cleaned and polished regularly, displayed in special jewelry cases, and polished and shined with special cloths. When we are in our purpose – we are respected and trusted. We have proven we belong there. God respects us, loves us and handles us with the utmost care. In your destined purpose, people will respect the anointing on your life, value your gift, and handle you with care. If they don't, there's no need to be upset with them, just remove you. Never devalue yourself to prove a point. You should always shine as GEWWELS. We are not responsible for how people treat us; we are only responsible for how we treat people and how we respond to unfair, unjust treatment.

When jewelry finds itself in the hands of a person who does not know how to care for, treat or respect it, it doesn't force itself on the individual, all it does is continue on in its natural purpose and that is to shine. If the individual does not handle the jewelry correctly, then ultimately the jewelry, never outside of its purpose, is misplaced or damaged. In the instance that it is lost, it's still shining, wherever it is, but not in its original purpose. Jewels never lose their purpose, but they can become dull, dusty, broken, or tarnished. With a little tender love and care, polish, and repair – it will be back to shining in its original state in no time. Sometimes that means with a new owner or partner.

Consider antique jewelry that has been passed down from one generation to the next. We see that this jewelry has served its purpose but has such a great value that it needs to keep being used in the lives of others. When taken to an antique jeweler the value on it can then be in the hundreds of thousands to millions. The same is true for us as His GEWWELS – what He has placed inside of us is to be shared from generation to generation. There are times when we will be mistreated, used and abused but this does not alter the point of our existence. We still have purpose. We can be repaired, healed, dusted off, polished, and put back into position to shine. It may not be with the person we thought it would be, it might not be the job or career we thought, but we will shine in purpose, on purpose for His purpose!

The route to our destination may change but our purpose will be fulfilled! We won't lose our luster; we will shine! We do shine! We are GEWWELS! Whatever or whoever caused us to detour in the beginning, or whoever lost us, or hurt us or devalued us, they are the ones at a lost, not us – our purpose will be fulfilled. It's time to get off the shelf in the display case – it's time to walk in our purpose! How do we get off the shelf, we stop fighting the process. How do we stop fighting the process, we embrace and endure the teaching, the corrections, the trials, the pain, the suffering; we stand on God's unchanging promises! We live according to His word and His plan. Furthermore, we stop fighting the God ordained leadership placed in our lives. We become teachable so we can learn and grow. We quiet ourselves to hear God. We learn God's word. We stop playing around with God and with church. We become about our Father's business.

In this book, we will discuss the process that the actual diamond and other jewelry go through in order to get to the display case and ultimately to its purpose. We will receive healing and deliverance in areas that were meant to shape and mold us, rather than crush and abuse us. We will see biblical examples of women who shined in purpose. We will learn of God's promises to us and make declarations to live accordingly. Your journey through this book will take you into a transparent view of my personal life but will ultimately thrust you into the place of your destiny in God. By the end of this book, you will have a new focus, new motivation, new strength, and new outlook on life. You will be ready to begin to shine in purpose on purpose for His purpose!

Introduction

All things work together for good to those who love God and are the called according to His purpose. Romans 8:28 (NKJV)

Strong's concordance states, diamond is from the Greek root word "Adamas" which means, unconquerable and indestructible. Diamonds are a testament of strength and endurance and the ultimate symbol of undying love. We as God's daughters are the same. We are a testament of strength and endurance and the ultimate symbol of God's undying love. His love first created us from the rib of man so that man would not be lonely. First point of purpose - He created us with a purpose in mind. His love sent Jesus into the world to live, die, and defeat death by rising from the dead to ascend back to heaven leaving us with power and authority in the earth. Jesus sacrifice gave us our salvation, our justification, and reconciled us back unto the Father after the fallen sins of mankind. Finally, His undying love gives us the opportunity to spend eternity with Him after leaving earth. Our strength and endurance are evident in our many accomplishments regardless of how we achieve it – most of our testimonies are that we made it! We find the strength to do what needs to be done and we endure the pain and the pressure.

Another example of strength and endurance that we do not share with the male gender is our ability to conceive, carry, birth, and mother a child. Moreover, for those who have not done it in the natural yet, you still have experienced the same strength and endurance by being able to carry, birth and mother in the spirit – where you are an aunt, godmother, step mother (I call us bonus moms, not step moms), friend, etc. You have impacted someone's life. The Bible tells us in Romans that we are more than conquerors therefore, we are unconquerable, we cannot be defeated. In the book of Luke the word tells us that nothing shall by any means hurt us, therefore, we are indestructible. As I said before the word diamond originally means unconquerable and indestructible, now you know how durable you are! God fashioned us after Himself – unconquerable and indestructible and considered it as priceless stone!
Each diamond is unique and each one reflects a story

of its journey from the depths inside the earth into treasured object of adornment. All diamonds share a certain feature that allows for comparison and differentiating them from one another. Our common feature is God. Our common feature is that we were created in the image and likeness of God. Our common feature is that we can stand on the same promises in His Word and it applies to each of us uniquely. The features in diamonds that differentiate them are called the 4 C's: Cut, Color, Clarity, and Carat Weight.

The Gemological Institute of America asserts, a diamonds cut unleashes its light. Diamonds are renowned for their ability to transmit (communicate, spread, transfer, convey) light and sparkle (excel, scintillate, shine, come into its own, stand out) so intensely. We often think of a diamond's cut as shape (round, emerald, pear), but that's not truth; a diamond's cut grade is about how well a diamond's facets (surfaces, sides, faces, features, aspects, issues, qualities) interact with light.

I think about this in relation to our existence in the earth. God created man and woman, He created them in His likeness, and in His image He created them both male and female. Since we were created in His image, we have the ability to transmit or communicate, spread, transfer, and convey His light – His word, His hope, His purpose, His good news, His joy, His peace, His love. Further, we have the ability to sparkle; to excel, come into our own purpose, and stand out from the rest, making an impact in the lives of others. We illuminate dark places, just because we were created in His image.

The GIA explains that the cut of the diamond is not related to is shape of round, emerald, pear, etc. rather the cut refers to how well the diamond's facets or faces, features, aspects, issues, or qualities interact with light. As this relates to us as God's GEWWELS we are not defined by our natural outer appearance of shape, size, color, ethnicity, background, family history, general curses, or educational lineage. These factors are important but they do not define us or place us in our destiny. What determines our outcome is our cut from the creator and how we interact with the Light! Jesus is the Light of the World. When God created the world, He spoke and said, "Let there be Light.". Light came and changed the world. Light brought peace and joy to the world.

Light opened our eyes to see. The Light brings forth new revelations. The Light sets things into proper prospective. The Light gives clear direction. We display how well we interact with the Light in our behaviors, our obedience, our trust in God, our faith, and in our reverence of the Light. We display how we interact with the Light in spoken words. We display how well we interact with the Light in how we treat people. Ask yourself now – what does my lifestyle say about how I interact with the Light? Ask yourself – do my actions say I am cut from the Almighty Creator or do my actions say I reflect the forces of evil? I've had to admit several times that my actions and attitude did not reflect Christ and therefore I needed to change. In order to shine in purpose, I needed to display His qualities at all times, not just when I was at church on Sunday or in Bible Study. My actions and attitude needed to be the same at the grocery store, at the child care facility, at work, when stewarding my finances, and handling bill collectors. The Light should be seen through us in every area of our life, at all times.

The GIA states, "A diamond's cut is crucial to the stone's final beauty and value." Precise artistry and workmanship are required to fashion a stone so its proportions, symmetry, and polish deliver the magnificent return of light only possible in a diamond. One thing I love about God is when He shaped us and fashioned us after His own image and likeness – He did it with us in mind. He knew how to perfectly place every organ in our body to make them magnificently perform together in their different proportions, symmetry, and final polishing. Your Cut is masterful – "Before I formed you in the womb I knew you; before you were born I sanctified you; I ordained you a prophet to the nations." (Jeremiah 1:5 KJV) The Bible declares that He knew us before He formed us in the womb. He already had the plan for us! We seem to forget that it was God who created us, not our mothers and fathers. God strategically placed every organ in the body, placed the call upon our life, and gave us breath. He is the Master Creator. Before you were conceived He had already sanctified you – that is – He already set you apart from evil, already set you apart from failure, already set you apart to succeed, and already set you apart for greatness. He uses the terms "ordained you a prophet to the nations," and this may not mean that you will be ordained by mankind as "prophet," but know He wants to use our voice to speak to many nations.

Let's take this book for example – this book is being used to edify, encourage, and inspire, God's people.

This book is being used to speak to the masses. No – I am not in the pulpit or going from country to country in the natural, but He is using the gift of writing and words to get His point across to many. The "many" can and will include those from other nations. Therefore, His word is being fulfilled – "I ordained you a prophet to the nations." I'm not giving myself a title of a prophet, but I'm allowing His perfect will to be done through my life. This is His desire for you as well. He set you apart with your specific God-given gift to edify the body of Christ and to change the body of unbelievers. Now, it is up to you to reveal how your qualities interact with the Light, which will ultimately reveal your final beauty and value. When considering your identity in terms of cut – remember that you were fearfully and wonderfully made by the Creator, not by society, not by the amount of money you have or don't have.

Finally, you must know that you are important! You are so important that the Cut Creator knows the very number of hairs on your head. That tells me that even when one or two hairs shed, He knows which ones are left and which ones He needs to replace. When society tries to make you feel irrelevant, like you do not exist, you must know and declare loudly, "I am important, so important that even the hairs on my head are numbered."

You are a rare cut and the price that was paid for your life is non replaceable! Out of all the four c's in the diamonds quality repertoire the cut is the most complex and technically difficult to analyze. This makes sense in terms of why people can never figure us out and why we are sometimes the recipients of slander and character assassinations. Our cut makes us unique and we do not fit in to the normal categories of life. When we do not fall in line with what people want us to look like or what they expect us to do or who they want us to be, then we receive criticism. However, it is because of our cut that we are complex individuals and we are not meant to be figured out! No one understands the mysteries of God, His sovereignty, His grace, His mercy, and His love; we can never figure Him out. It is true then for us. Continue on shining in purpose on purpose for His purpose...You are cut from the Creator!

Color[1]

GIA's education on diamonds teaches that a diamonds color actually means "lack of color." The diamond color evaluation of most gem-quality diamonds is based on the absence of color. A chemically pure and structurally perfect diamond has no hue, like a drop of pure water, and consequently, a higher value.[1] This is a WOW moment as we relate the diamond process with our life process. The diamond's lack of color is what gives it its meaning, its value, its importance, and its rank.

As God's GEWWELS what determines our meaning in life, our value, our success, our eternity is an invisible hue of the shed blood of Jesus on the Cross. It is this blood that no one sees in the natural, but it gives us life. It's the blood that cleanses us; it's the blood that protects us from hurt, harm, and danger. The shed blood of Jesus washed away our guilt and sin. The blood of Jesus puts us back in right position with the Father and gives us access to eternal life in heaven. This invisible color of red is our life-line. We plead the blood of Jesus and rest in security, and peace, knowing all is well. The invisible red gives each of us in our individualities the same common denominator of life and life more abundantly. This invisible red, crystalizes our life and makes us stand out to others. This invisible red attracts nonbelievers to the Light of the World. This invisible red defeats demons and forces of evil that try to infiltrate our lives. When we apply the blood of Jesus to situations and circumstances we exalt Jesus and we declare victory. Miracles manifest through this invisible red. We are to stand firm on the blood of Jesus knowing that it is His blood that paved the way for us over 2000 years ago, but it is still tangibly miraculous today.

The lack of color seen in our lives is what gives us our life! Our identity is not according to what we have tangibly on the outside, it is determined by the acceptance of Jesus as Lord and Savior, the belief that He died and rose for our salvation and the application of the invisible hue of red that He naturally shed for us. Although it is not seen with the natural eye, the blood of Jesus is our identity. It is the blood of Jesus that makes us a chosen generation, and a royal priesthood. Apply the blood, use the blood, plead the blood, although it's not seen by others, it makes you shine!

Clarity[1]

According to GIS, a diamond's clarity refers to the absence of inclusions and blemishes. I like this. This says that what defines a diamond's clarity is what is no longer present or relevant. This tells me that somewhere along the line there were some marks and blemishes but those marks and blemishes don't define the jewel, it is the absence of the blemishes, or the absence of what was believed to be included. The inclusions refer to some internal characteristics that result from tremendous heat and pressure. Some of the internal characteristics that would like to gain claim of our life's direction and outcome include family history, legacies, accidents, hurt and pain, lack, rejection, health issues, marriage failures, abuse, etc. These internal characteristics were designed to leave permanent external characteristic called blemishes. However, when Jesus died for our sins, He made the internal issues absent by taking it to the cross; He covered the external blemishes or scars with His blood and manifested the Fruit of the Spirit as result.

Therefore, as God's GEWWELS, the absence of those internal and external characteristics is what gives us our clarity. Our new manifestation is the Fruit of the Spirit. Instead of walking in condemnation, we walk in freedom; instead of being hurt, we walk in love, joy, and peace. Instead of seeing revenge, we walk in faithfulness, goodness, and self-control. God does not see what our family history is; He is only concerned with His plan for your life. His thoughts towards you do not include your family history of lack, poverty, sickness and disease, premature death, dysfunctional homes, or mediocrity.

The clarity for the path of your life is determined in the absence of the internal inclusions and the absence of the external blemishes. You may have experienced it, but it does not navigate your life's destiny. No diamond is perfectly pure, yet the closer it comes to perfection, the higher its value. I encourage you to continue to grow in the faith and continue to follow God. He is not looking for perfection in accordance to Webster's dictionary definition, "a person or thing that is the perfect embodiment of some quality" but perfection in terms of maturity – growing in Him, allowing Him to orchestrate your life, giving Him complete control of your destiny. This is how you get to the level of clarity where things are absent to the natural eye. It's then we shout – you don't know my story, all you see is the glory. The clarity of God's GEWWELS is apparent when the glory of God is made manifest in our life.

Carat Weight[1]

A Diamond's carat weight is the measurement of how much a diamond weighs. Although each has a similar process to endure to reach its stage for polishing, the diamonds may not weigh the same. The overall process contains the same methods, but each diamond experiences different amounts of pressure, cutting, heat, and polishing to get to its purposeful shape and size. The same is true for us as God's GEWWELS. The overall process may contain many of the same methods like the process of conception and birth, being raised from adolescence to adulthood, attending schools, etc., but beyond that each of our life's circumstances are different and have a different effect on us.

Let's take me for example – I grew up with my natural dad until I was 7 years old and then he transitioned from this life; beyond that I lived with a stepdad, in the rough part of St. Louis City, with very little money and my mom was afflicted with sickness so she could not work. I experienced sexual abuse, verbal abuse, sibling rivalry, and had to work hard to fit in during elementary school. I was struck by a car, had to spend many nights without food and utilities; and the list goes on. These things happened before the age of 18.

A lot of these circumstances, I had no control over because I was a child. Then, as I continued to grow up, I started creating my own issues and practicing different sins. I entered wrong relationships, started drinking alcohol, skipped school, and lied constantly, all while attending the local church. Yes, I had verbally given my life to Jesus, but my actions did not align with what my heart knew was right. All the circumstances I experienced, whether of my own doing or from childhood, contributed to my carat weight. These situations were equivalent to pressure, heat, cutting, and polishing in the diamond making process. In the actual process of diamond making, the price increases with diamond carat weight. The price for my life and the circumstances that shaped it were too expensive to make me pay for – therefore, Jesus took all of it with Him to the cross when He was crucified. His crucifixion is the ultimate carat weight because He took it all upon Himself.. He took the pressure, the heat, the cutting, and the polishing and finished our life's future outcome for us so that we do not have to worry about the cost. With His sacrifice we are no longer consumed with the weight of our life's situations. We know that sin is heavy, life circumstances are heavy, lost is heavy, and the process is heavy. Yet we don't have to carry it!

Moreover, the anointing on your life is heavy, but it shall not weigh you down. When the heaviness seems unbearable, we are instructed to put on the garment of praise for the spirit of heaviness. Jesus has instructed us to cast our cares (weights, circumstances, situations, issues) on Him. We were never expected to carry heavy weight, so let it go, get it off of you. God's answer to the heaviness of the carat weight is Jesus. Jesus' answer to the heaviness of life's carat weight is praise. It's important to remember that a diamond's value is determined using all of the 4Cs, not just carat weight.

Let's look at a biblical example of a woman who

shined in purpose, on purpose for His purpose. Mary, the mother of Jesus, is our example of a girl who entered womanhood while experiencing life's struggles.

Luke 1:26-38 (NKJV) "Now in the sixth month the angel Gabriel was sent by God to a city of Galilee called Nazareth, to a virgin betrothed to a man whose name was Joseph of the house of David. The virgins name was Mary. And having come in the angel said to her "Rejoice highly favored one, the Lord is with you, blessed are you among women. But when she saw him she was troubled at his saying and considered what manner of greeting this was. Then the angel said to her "Do not be afraid Mary for you have found favor with God. And behold you will conceive in your womb and bring forth a Son and shall call His name Jesus. He will be great and will be called the Son of the Highest and the Lord God will give Him the throne of his father David. And He will reign over the house of Jacob forever end of His kingdom there will be no end." Then Mary said to the angel "How can this be since I do not know a man?" And the angel answered and said to her "The Holy Spirit will come upon you and the power of the

Highest will overshadow you; therefore, also that Holy One who is to be born will be called the Son of God. Now indeed Elizabeth your relative has also conceive a son in her old age and this is now the 6 months of her who was called barren. For with God nothing will be impossible. Then Mary said "Behold the maid servant of the Lord, let it be to me according to your word" and the angel departed from her.

"Let it be to me according to your word." These words speak volume about Mary, about her faith, about her trust, about her humility, and about her purpose. The first thing that we notice is that Mary was called to serve God at an early age she was called even before she was married. God called Mary into her purpose while she was still in her purity (a virgin). It is in our purity that we see better, hear better, and trust easier. In purity – contamination from the outside environment or cultural substances have not infiltrated or destroyed our thinking, our hope, or our course especially when we are already in Christ. Many GEWWELS received their calling during purity but many are not able to reach their point of purpose at a young age because of environmental and cultural influences. Often times, our gifts manifest during childhood schooling, whether it's a like or thirst for academics, medicine, design, dance, praying, helping others, playing music, sports, singing, etc. Then, family life or peer pressure leads us away from our destiny.

Truth is – just because individuals in your family are either addicted to drugs or alcohol, parties and clubs all the time, live in poverty, or lives a fantasy life, does not mean that is the same final result for you. You can decide to live according to God's design and plan for your life and not follow the historical pattern of failure seen through your family's generations. It is ok to accept the call of God on your life at an early age. Just think of how many lives will be affected when you do. It is ok to start a business in your youth, it is ok to write a book as a child, or start a clothing line. You are not too young for God to bless the work of your hands. It is also true for those who are receiving their calling in their later years – it is not too late. In the book of Kings, there was a widow who used jars in her house to pay her debts and then live on. God wants to use us in whatever stage of life we are in. Mary just accepted in her purity.

During this cultural time, to be pregnant and not married was shunned upon. Mary knew that if she was found to be pregnant before marriage it would put her and her family in the line of fire for ridicule and possibly even a death penalty. With Mary being in the position where she could be stoned to death she decided not to succumb to peer pressure or people pleasing. She, with her childlike faith, boldly and firmly declared "let it be to me according to Your Word." When this is our declaration we will see more of God's Word manifested in our life, we will see more proof of His promises, and we will see more Fruit of the Spirit operating in our daily lives. We must make this saying a part of our daily vocabulary; "Lord let it be to me according to your Word." We must declare the wealth of the wicked is stored up for the righteous - let it be done to me according to your word. I am the head and not the tail - let it be done to me according to Your word. He knows the plans He has for me - let it be unto me according to His word.

The blessings of the Lord make us rich and adds no sorrow - let it be done to me according to Your word. He will rebuke the devour for my namesake - let it be into me according to Your word. He came that we might have life and have it more abundantly - let it be done to me according to

Your word. The Lord is my Shepherd I shall not want - let it be done to me according to Your word. I trampled over scorpions and serpents and nothing shall by any means hurt me - let it be done to me according to Your Word. No good thing will He withhold from those who walk upright - let it be done to me according to Your word. Goodness and mercy shall follow me all the days of my life and I shall dwell in the house of the Lord forever – let it be done to me according to Your word. He will perfect everything that concerns me – let it be done to me according to Your word.

The key is to know the promises of God, find the promise for your circumstance and declare that is will be done unto you according to His Word. What did God say about your business? Well, let it be done to you according to His Word. What did He say about health? Well, let it be done to you according to His Word. What did the man or woman of God prophesy over your life? Let it be done to you according to His Word. It's His Word, it's His promise, and He will keep it. You do your part and watch Him manifest

His.

Additionally, Mary was engaged when she received her call and purpose from the Lord. This meant her plans were interrupted for God's Will to be fulfilled. Since she surrendered her will to God and allowed His perfect to manifest, God blessed and increased her more. Remember the angel from God told her she had found favor with God. God cannot lie; favor means just that – favor. This favor held her relationship together with Joseph. This favor protected her when her life was in danger. This favor gave her a place to birth the baby when all doors were shut. This favor graced her to raise a holy anointed child according to God's Will and His Word. Favor is just that – favor.

There comes a time in our lives when we must fully surrender our will and plan to the Lord and allow His plan to be birthed in and through us. In order to totally surrender we must trust in the word of the Lord from Romans 8:28, that all things work together for good to those who love God and are the called according to His purpose. In this we find that favor is manifested in our life. Although it does not make us exempt from struggle or pain, we are favored to come through it untouched like the three Hebrew boys who were in the midst of the fire, but not consumed, not touched, there was not even a stench of fire on them. They too were favored.

Mary and Joseph were no doubt in love with one another, but what's even more important is that they both loved God. Mary didn't need to tell the angel that she was engaged, all she needed to do was give her *yes* and God took care of the rest. Where there is a yes to His Will, there is liberty to complete it without hesitation, hindrance, or confusion as long as we stay true to His plan. Will obstacles come, yes, but His vision and plans always come with provision. Stay the course; trust His plan even when it does look like you see His hand working.

I recall once when the Holy Spirit told me to get in the car and drive two hours away to Jefferson City to sign some paperwork. The issue was that I had not spoken with my husband about it because he was at work and his cell phone was not working. Trusting God, I got in the truck and hopped on the highway. I stopped to fill up the gas tank. While pumping the gas, my husband calls me and says, "I think you need to go to Jeff City today – can you put gas in the truck and head there?" I responded to let him know I was already at the gas station getting gas and was in route. God is not the author of confusion. And when you are in His divine plan He will speak to both or all parties involved. All He needs is your yes! We must keep our trust in God, trust the leading of the Holy Spirit and know that all things work together so that you shine in purpose, on purpose for His purpose.

Mary's purpose was to be the chosen vessel to bring the Messiah into the earthly realm. Her mission included raising Him and caring for Him in accordance to Holy Scripture and God's instruction. This was a huge job that Mary needed to fulfill but we don't see in the much in the scriptures about Mary. The focus is not on Mary. As a matter of fact, she only really gets recognized once a year and that is around Christmas time, when we celebrate the birth of Christ The truth is we cannot talk about the birth of Christ without talking about His mother. She does not get praise on Mother's Day and there are no special days set aside for her. Yet, Mary lived her life in danger and agony, as she had to constantly protect Jesus, cover Him, and even move Him from city to city. She had to know when to be His mom and when to be His submissive follower. Although she did not receive much recognition, Mary had an extremely important purpose. It did not make her naturally wealthy, but she had a purpose. No matter how great or small the assignment, we must be willing to do it with every fiber of our being for the sake of the Kingdom of God.

In God's eyes Mary shined in purpose. He kept her covered and protected; He sent her warnings when danger was approaching. God loved Mary very much and He knew before she was born what He would use her for in the Kingdom. The same is true for us today. He loves us with a love that is non comprehensible and He created each one of us for a different purpose here in the earth that will maximize the Kingdom of God.

The angel Gabriel told Mary exactly what God was going to accomplish. He told her that she was chosen and highly favored. Then, he gave her some specifics like "His name shall be called Jesus!" God is still sending His people comfort, instructions, and specifics according to and regarding His plan for our daily living. Do not think it strange when you receive instructions and they do not line up with what the world says or what appears to be normal. His ways are not our ways; His thoughts are not our thoughts. His ways will normally be supernatural with a natural manifestation.

When the Lord sent me the message that I would have a baby boy, I was elated to say the least. He sent me specific instructions and guidelines to follow; He even sent us a messenger to tell us his name. He fulfilled His promise to us and exactly when He told me to take the pregnancy test is exactly when it showed positive. January 2011, He told me, "Isaac will come forth this year." In July 2011, we did IVF (invitro-fertilization) and it failed. I was devastated. After repenting for putting my hands in the process, I released the desire to have a child to the Lord and sincerely said "I will serve You with a child and I will serve You even if I never have a child." I began to enjoy life and then in October 2011, He reminded me of His promise to bring Isaac forth this year. December 12, 2011, I heard the Holy Spirit instruct me to take a pregnancy test on Christmas day. I tried to ignore what I was hearing and I never mentioned it to anyone. On Christmas eve, as we were preparing for bed, after saying our prayers, my husband leaned over to give me a good night kiss and I almost threw up. He stepped back and said, "So, I make you sick?" And my awkward response was "um, apparently, I guess so." I knew at that moment, I needed to take a pregnancy test.

On Christmas morning, I battled back and forth in my mind about taking this test. It was Christmas morning, on a Sunday, and I would be the only minister in Children's Church because the other minister was on vacation. I did not want to be sad with all those children on Christmas morning trying to discuss the miraculous birth of our Savior. I told the Lord, "no, I cannot take this test today." After going back and forth with the Lord for ten minutes, He won and I took the test. However, I turned the test upside down on the side of the bathtub so I could not see the results. After a few minutes, I muscled up enough nerves to pick the stick up and look at it. When I looked at the stick, I couldn't believe what I was seeing; two lines instead of just one. I grabbed the instructions from the box and read what it meant because I was in total shock. It was 6:00 AM, Christmas morning. I slowly walk into our bedroom and woke my husband. I told him that I took a pregnancy test and I needed him to look at it with me to make sure that I was seeing what I thought I was seeing. When he looked at it, he did exactly what I did, grabbed the instructions to see what it meant. Then, he looked at me with the grandest smile and said, "You're Pregnant!" Well, Merry Christmas to us! God kept His promise...Isaac came forth in 2011. It was not the way I intended. I thought, with my limited wisdom, that when He spoke that to me in January that it meant Isaac would be born in 2011.

It is imperative that when God speaks to us, we hear what He says and not what we want Him to say. When He sends you the Word to start this million-dollar business, write this series of books, prepare for a child (when your natural body says different), or relocate to do ministry, just respond "let it be done unto me according to Your Word," follow His instructions, and experience the blessings of His spoken word. Don't read any more into His Word and don't take anything away from His Word. When sickness tries to afflict your body or plague your family, just respond "let healing be done unto me according to Your Word." In the natural, Mary's answer was a simple yes, but actually her response was life changing. Your yes to God will change your life; it will change the course of your life. When you say yes to God do not expect things to remain the same. A songwriter sings, "Your yes could cost you everything." That may be true, but your yes will in return get you more than what you had before. The principle is you cannot beat God giving. You give Him a yes, He gives you life, He gives you abundance, and He gives you a guaranteed victory! We must respond yes to His will with thorough knowledge and understanding of the principles and promises He has set forth in His Word. Jesus' yes cost Him His life but it gave us life! Imagine how your yes can help someone or change the world.

In the remaining segments of this book, we will walk through some of the issues that attempt to hinder us from shining in purpose.

Chapter 1 - Childhood

At an early age I learned that the word of God is true. One of the scriptures that stood out to me was, *"the thief comes but to steal, to kill, and to destroy, but I came that you might have life and have it more abundantly."* John 10:10.

I would like to say that my childhood was a pleasant time, but the truth is my childhood was a rough and treacherous. What is awesome about it is that you cannot tell by looking at me that I had a rough upbringing. One month before my 8th birthday, my daddy passed away. I was not certain what my sister meant when she sat me in the back of the red truck and said, "Cha Cha, you won't see daddy again until you get to heaven." At 7 years old, I didn't know much about heaven, so my response was, "OK, where is heaven, can we go now?" With tears in her eyes, she explained that we couldn't go now it was not our time. This is the time I remember my life turning to a quick down fall.

Before Daddy passed, I was the epitome of a daddy's girl. I remember being the only child in daycare everyday with 2 white castles with no onions and no cheese, because Daddy always said we couldn't afford the cheese. If I go to White Castles today I still order them the same way. I remember Daddy being pulled over by the police one morning as he was taking me to kindergarten. They arrested him and took him to the police station. With all the love in his heart, he asked the officers if I could sit outside the cell while he was inside the cell because he did not want his daughter to be behind bars. He also asked them if they could share their donuts with me because we had not had a chance to stop for breakfast yet; and the officers complied with his request.

After it was all over, they released him and he proceeded to take me to school. My daddy loved me and I knew it. I am the first born to the union of my mother and father. My parents wanted children together but were told that my mom could not have anymore (she had my eldest sister when she was 16). After a 21-year wait, the Lord touched my mother's body and she conceived. I am their miracle child and Daddy made sure to treat me as such. My eldest sister always reminds me that when I was born, Daddy held me up in his arms and said, "This is my queen, and she is going to change this world." I remember while my family lived in the Vaughn housing projects in St. Louis, MO, my cousin and I were coming from the community center and a man was trying to snatch me. My cousin held her ground and fought for me. When we finally made it back to the apartment, we told the security and we told my daddy.

Daddy went on a long search for this man and I knew if he had found him, it would not have been a great ending for that man. When I broke my arm, Daddy stayed at the hospital with me and cried because he was not there when I fell. Yes, I was the epitome of a daddy's girl! The truth is that while he was a super dad to me, he and mom did not get along so well. There was another family involved and I had sisters and brothers that did not live with me. I remember mom sitting us children down (because after me my mom had two more girls – giving her a total of four girls) and she explained that we were going to talk to a judge and the judge was going to ask us, who we wanted to live with, her or daddy. She asked what we were going to say and I joyfully spurted out, "I'm going to live with my daddy!" This must have broken my mom's heart because she responded, "If he wanted your silly butt he would be here with you, but he don't want you – he is there with them." I didn't know or understand what they were going through, but I loved my daddy and whenever I was at his "other" house I had a lot of fun because there were so many more children, we played all the time.

My parents were scheduled to get a divorce on the first Tuesday in May in 1986, but he passed away on that Sunday before the court hearing. This caused my life to go into a constant whirlwind. From that point on, life threw me tough blows. Shortly, after his death, I was staying with a family member and one of the boys forced me to have intercourse with him and threatened to hurt me if I ever said anything. I remember sitting there crying and saying, "I want my daddy," but daddy could not come rescue me.

My mom was afflicted with epilepsy and we were warned not to cause her worry because she could have a seizure and die; so I didn't tell mom about what was happening because I didn't want her to go to heaven too. These acts of sexual abuse continued from the age of 8 to the age of 11. I was terrified and never wanted to go visit family, but mom needed a break and these were our baby sitters. I wanted the acts to stop, but I didn't know how to stop them. So I stopped taking baths before I went to their house. I thought that if I were stinky, they would not touch me. It worked for a while until they began to tell their sisters to make me take a bath. So the girls would put me in the tub and make me bathe. I hated it! The worst part of all of this is that when I was 16 I went to the doctor for a checkup and they did a pap smear and found that I had a contracted an STD and that I had had it for a while. All I could think was I want my daddy. After confrontation between mom and the family sitters, we finally stopped going over there and I was relieved.

Daddy's death brought on a lot of confrontation in our household. There was sibling rivalry all the time. I found it difficult to get along with one of my sisters. We grew up with much dislike for one another. From my viewpoint, she had more of my mom's attention, more of her love and more of her care. I longed to have mom love me like the love she displayed for my sister.. After daddy left, I didn't' get to celebrate my birthday anymore because we never had money for me to get a cake or ice cream and definitely not any gifts. However, when my sister's birthday came around she always had cake and ice cream and even friends came over to celebrate with her. This conceived a huge jealousy within me. I didn't understand at the time that mom was on a fixed income because of her physical disability. Money was always tight around my birthday because by the end of the month there was no money. My sister's birthday fell on the day when we got the once a month checks so mom was able to get her cake and ice cream. Yet in my adolescent mind, I was not loved because I didn't get to celebrate my birthday. Most times, mom would forget it was my birthday. Even when I was an adult living on my own, my baby sister would call mom and say, "today is Cha Cha birthday don't forget to call her momma."

To know that it was easy for her to forget my birthday was a cut inside of me that took a long while to heal. Ultimately, what I learned from these issues from my childhood was to make sure to plan. I became very organized and detailed and I gained a love for celebrations. To this day, I take time to plan so that nothing goes unnoticed or undone. Every year I make a list of the upcoming celebrations for the next year with the dates and I begin to prepare 3 to 4 months in advance. For example, I know that every year Christmas is celebrated on December 25, therefore instead of waiting until November to start shopping, I begin in August. I do the same for birthdays, anniversaries, etc. It's a wise idea to make planning a part of the process of your life. No we are not attempting to please everyone, but if we make an effort to let someone know you love and appreciate them, it will speak volumes in their life and it will set you up for harvest reaping. There is a universal divine law of reciprocity that scripture refers to as sowing and reaping. When you do for others, you will receive in return.

My mother's boyfriend lived with us and it made things horrible. He made it known that he didn't like me. He and Mom were in agreement about not liking me. Several times, my mom would say to me, "I cannot stand you – you look just like your daddy, you act like him, you walk like him, and when you grow up, you are going to be a whore just like him." These words made me grow cold toward my mom. With every negative word she spoke about dad, my heart grew colder. The man living with us did not work, all he did was sit around the house and watch television and this frustrated me. My mom was on a fixed income that came once a month. Because of this, there was always a shortage in food and I could not comprehend why this man was in our home eating up food and doing nothing to make sure we had more. There were three growing girls in this home and a woman who needed certain foods because of diabetes and epilepsy. I grew angry toward him. In my young mind, this was not how life was supposed to be. We were not able to get new clothes and shoes when needed and there were many times when we were without lights, gas, phone, and even water in our home because there was no money.

I later learned that the man living with us was heavily addicted to drugs and he would take money from the house to feed his habit. It went on for a while until mom got tired of it, but her frustration didn't really set in until we began to go to church. There was one time we had absolutely nothing in the house and it was cold outside. My eldest sister, who is 21 years older than me, came to get us and take us to her house for a few days until things were better. I witnessed the "things" she had and I knew I wanted to live life like her. She had a car, we did not; she had lots of nice clothes, we did not; she had a beautiful home, we did not; she had a full refrigerator, we did not; she had a job, and I wanted one. I began to admire my older sister and I wanted to live like she did. After this episode in our own home, my eldest sister began to come around more and I could see a glimmer of hope for my own life.

To witness this man in our home not putting in or helping us and witnessing how we had to do without, I made up in my mind that I would always work to support myself and I would never depend on a man to take care of me. The downfall of this kind of attitude is that it made me so independent that I didn't even depend on God who is THE Jehovah Jireh our Provider. Sometimes we take our ambitions so far that we eliminate God. That is not what He wanted me to learn from this situation. What He wanted me to learn is how to manage money, how to be a good steward over what He had given me. He wanted me to learn the importance of being in covenant relationship with the godly man He created me to be with, and not some random man who I was only physically attracted to. He wanted me to learn to wait on Him. He wanted me to learn that when you are not equally yoked in relationships, you set yourself up for the effects of the cankerworm, palmerworm, locust, etc. to cut off your supply and destroy your peace. On a positive note, I did learn how important it was for me to take education serious and I learned that nothing was going to just be given to me, that I needed to work hard to accomplish the desired goals I wanted to achieve.

Finally, I learned that my mother did the best she knew how to do and I love her and appreciate all she did for me. I appreciate what she was not able to do for me because it taught me how to be a better woman. Her inevitable inabilities taught me positive life lessons because I knew I never wanted to live like how I grew up and I was determined that when I had children of my own, I would do my best to provide a loving, nurturing, and teaching environment. Now, as an adult, my mother and I have the best relationship ever and I'm grateful that she is still here with me. I forgave her a long time ago and I told her how I felt about the way we grew up. I released those feelings and emotions. She confessed to me that she only did what her mother did to her and she apologized. I forgave my mom because I love her, I forgave my mom because she is my mom, I forgave my mom so I could have peace in my heart and not anger. I forgave my mom because Christ forgave me.

When I was 11 years old, I was coming home from school and a car struck me. The impact of the accident threw me several hundred feet in the air and when I came down I bounced on top of the car three times before rolling off into the street. I didn't even know I was hit because I got up out the street and walked to the sidewalk. All the bystanders were totally surprised. My books were on the nearest side street and my shoes were sitting in the sewer. My ponytail had come down and I was a little dizzy. The driver of the school bus called out to me and told me to sit down and wait for the ambulance that was on the way.

The police arrived with my mom and stepdad and the ambulance took me away. I was not in pain that day, but the next day, I was in a lot of pain and could barely move my leg. This accident brought on a whole new longing for my daddy. At the time, I wasn't interested in simply giving God praise that I was still able to walk. At 11 years old, I was focused on how I would now have to wear this ugly mechanical brace on my leg for the rest of my life because the ligaments in my knee were torn. I felt even more fear grip me, as I knew children would tease me and talk about me more than they already did. I knew my activities were limited and I would have to fight to have genuine friends in my life that would not judge me or treat me bad because of my situation. My life had truly taken a turn.

My eldest sister and her family began going to church. They told Mom they were going to church and I pleaded to go with her. She allowed us to go with her one Sunday. This Sunday morning, I wore the only dress I owned and I was happy to go. I didn't know much about church, but it sounded good. I remembered going when daddy was alive and the few times that grandma would take us when we were younger. After the preacher preached, he said, "The doors of the church are open." He stood at the front of the church with his arms open wide and began to say all these beautiful things about Jesus. He said "Jesus will make your life brand new, He will take care of you, come to Jesus." I thought to myself...WOW He will do all that. I wanted a new life; I needed a new life. I needed someone to take care of me and I wanted what he was offering. I looked at my sister and asked if I could go up there and she was apprehensive but finally she said yes. I went to the front with my other little sister, and we joined the church, we gave our life to Jesus. The preacher said, "Did you know that Jesus loves you?" I said, "No." He said, "Yes He does, and He died on the cross so you could have a better life with Him in heaven." I thought to myself, heaven that sounds familiar; I want to go there, that is where my daddy is, so I was sold. Whatever he told me I needed to do I was doing it because I had to get to where my daddy was. Plus I wanted this new life because in my mind mine was not a very happy one.

We were officially candidates for baptism and they gave us a day to tell our mom that we were getting baptized. When we got home I was excited to tell Momma that we'd joined church. When we walked in the door, she was sitting in her famous chair by the window, rocking back and forth. I said, "Momma, guess what." As she wiped tears from her eyes, she said, "Y'all joined church," and she broke down crying. I looked at my eldest sister confused. Then Momma told us that while she was in the kitchen cooking dinner, the Lord told her that her kids joined church today. Our baptism was scheduled for a couple of weeks later following our join date. On the day we were baptized, our mother came to church to see us get baptized and she joined the church too. On that day, our mother witnessed 3 of her 4 daughters (the baby girl was too small), her only 2 grandsons, and her only son-in-law (at the time) all get baptized together. It was a family affair, a day of jubilee, and a day of change for our family. I thank God for my eldest sister! I know she was a bit reluctant in the beginning because we did not have transportation to get back and forth to church and that would have been a heavy strain on her.

However, because of her obedience to take us and allow us to join, God has done marvelous, miraculous things in our lives. I would not be where I am in Christ today if she would have said no to us joining the church. The church had a church van and we were able to prevent being a burden on her. All God needs is one willing vessel to say yes. He doesn't need us to do much more than say yes. He knows the plans He has for us and He uses His earthly vessels to accomplish these plans. I admonish you to allow God to use you to help others get to their destiny and pay attention when He is using others to assist you. Be discerning but trust God's hand when it comes to the plan of your life.

Our stories may be different in circumstance, but the truth is many of us have tough childhood experiences that have helped to shape us into the women (young or old) we are today. I initially dealt with the loss of a parent at a young age. Loss or death of a parent or loved one at any age is tough. This is also true of loss through divorce. If you are young when it occurs, then there is a chance of growing up living in fear, resentment, bitterness, people pleasing, jealousy/envy, anger, and hurt. What's happening in this situation is that abandonment is taking root in your life. We are not in control of what God does when He calls someone home to be with Him. We are not responsible if parents decide to divorce. Growing up without one or both parents is difficult, but once we learn to put our trust in God we can learn to experience Him as the parent we are missing.

Let me be clear here. As time went on in my life and I developed a closer relationship with Jesus, I learned to depend on Him to comfort me. I learned to look to Him when I was lost, hurting, or confused. No, my actual dad was no longer present, but God filled the emptiness I felt in my heart. Since age 18, God began to celebrate my birthday. Every year on my birthday there is always a special blessing He gives me that no one else can do. After the car struck me, there was an annuity settlement set up for me. Every year on my birthday beginning at age 18 I received a check in the mail for $5,000 and I knew it was a blessing from God! What the devil meant for bad, God turned it around and used it to bless me. Even though daddy was not here to celebrate with me and Momma would forget or she never had money to celebrate my birthday, God made sure I knew that He did not forget and that I was special to Him.

Still, every year on my birthday, God does something very special for me. It has extended now even to Christmas celebrations. He lets me know how important I am to Him. I don't know whom you have lost in your life, but I encourage you to release them from your spirit so you can heal and receive of God. The spirit of grief will keep you from receiving the blessings of the Lord. It will keep you focused on something you have no control over. God wants you to experience the goodness of His love and favor and you cannot receive with your hands tightly holding on to what is no longer here. Release so you can receive.

God wants to heal you today from the strong man of abandonment. The enemy has conceived it in your mind that you have been abandoned by love ones, but God says, "I will never leave you nor forsake you." He has not left you! He is always with you even when it seems like He is not present. Jesus understands what it feels like to feel abandonment. He felt abandoned on the cross when He cried out, "My God, My God, why has Thou forsaken me." The truth is God had not abandoned Him, Jesus was His One true Son that He was well pleased with, and so God did not forsake Him. What happened to Jesus and what happens to us is that some very difficult painful situations must occur in order for us to fulfill our purpose.

As a GEWWEL, a girl entering womanhood while experiencing life's struggles, you will encounter painful situations to fulfill your purpose. Experience it, learn from it, and let it shape you! The enemy is interested in distorting your destiny from your birth because he knows you will be a force to be reckoned with in the spirit. He knows when you see how God can use you and you experience the abundance God has for you then he has lost the battle. His job is to infiltrate all these issues in your life at an early age and have you to focus on the negative side of them. I'm here to encourage you to see the positive in circumstances and situations because if you ever read the bible you will learn WE WIN! We are victorious! Satan loses. Where will you be when the battle is over shining in purpose or defeated in dust? You are a GEWWEL created to *shine in purpose*!

Chapter 2 - Family

In Psalm 51, David, speaking to the Lord, says, "Blot out my transgressions, wash me thoroughly from my iniquity, and cleanse me from my sin. For I acknowledge my transgression and my sin is always before me. Behold, I was brought forth in iniquity and in sin my mother conceived me. Behold, You desire truth in the inward parts and in the hidden part You will make me to know wisdom. Purge me with hyssop and I shall be clean; wash me and I shall be whiter than snow. Hide your face from my sins and blot out all my iniquities (Psalm 51:1-3; 5-7; 9). David was not a perfect man but was considered a man after God's own heart. God looks at the heart of person, not only at the actions of a person. In the Psalm, David was calling out in a prayer of repentance. He was repenting for his actions, which derived from his own decisions, but also he was repenting from actions that occurred from his ancestral lineage, which is known as transgressions. The Bible gives us different words for sin and it is imperative to know the difference so that you will know how to pray and how to repent. Let's begin with "chattah" a Hebrew word that means, "missing the mark" (Strongs 2403). Every one of us falls into this category of sin because we all miss the mark, whether it's intentional or accidental. To better understand missing the mark we will look at the example of an archer. An archer uses a bow and arrow to hit the bull's-eye on a target. He pulls the bow back and released the arrow and it hits a spot on the target board. When he hits exactly what he was aiming for then he has accomplished his goal, but if the arrow hits anything other than the target, then he has missed the mark. He had well intentions of reaching his goal, but even in all his trying, he missed it. It was not planned to miss it, but it happened. That is what happens when we "chattah," we aim at doing right but then somehow we miss it a bit. Remember we all sin and fall short of the glory of God (Romans 3:23). For this reason, there is now therefore no condemnation to those who love God and are in God. We are not expected to be perfect in the sense of blameless. We are expected to not practice wrongdoing. When we practice in wrongdoing then we move into a sin pattern that is either from a transgression or an iniquity. When we have knowingly broken a rule that has been established then we fall into transgression or the Hebrew word "pesha." Then, finally, when we find ourselves in habit of wrongdoing and this wrongdoing is causing harm to oneself or others, it is usually something you can trace from other family members, we are then in iniquity or "avown." Avown is the wrongdoing that is within our innermost being. Iniquity is passed through the bloodline mostly of the father. This is the number one reason why the Holy Spirit impregnated Mary, because although Joseph was a good man, his blood was still contaminated because he was human.

David understood that he desired to live a life please to God, but sometimes his actions were against biblical standards. He understood that he was born with the nature to sin, and yet even more disturbing to him, he understood that some of what he experienced was from the result of his family lineage. This Psalm displays his heartfelt repentance for what he did in his flesh from his own choices, but also we see his heartfelt repentance for the iniquities that were manifested through his bloodline.. When he could not control himself enough to prevent falling into adultery and murder, he knew he was struggling with a stronghold that had been passed down from generation to generation. Many of us find ourselves in the same situations. We desire to do right but evil is always present. Sin is always crouching at the door waiting for us to open it so sin can enter. The great news is we don't have to succumb to the sin that is waiting for us; we can walk in deliverance from the family lineage of generational curses. We can begin to experience generational blessings. This process is one more testament of what helps to shape us into the beautiful GEWWELS God has created us to be. He wants to use you to stop the madness of iniquity that has plagued your family. He does not want another generation to endure such inner discomfort. He wants you and your children and children's children to the 7th and 8th generation to understand His love, His care, His prosperity, His peace, and His freedom.

I experienced a terrible warfare with witchcraft from 2008-2010. The doctors could not figure out what was going on in my body. I was struggling severely with menstrual bleeding. It was so bad many times I could not leave the house . What truly made the situation worse was I was a married woman and I had been bleeding for nearly 2 years straight without a break. Imagine the strain this cause on my marriage –

financially and emotionally. To make matters worse, I began to experience fevers, my temperature would rise to 99.9 and I would shake and tremble uncontrollably but the temperature would never reach 100. The doctors were confused because every test they ran returned normal but it was clear that my body was dying. Scratching his head, the doctor said, "I'm at a loss for words." They treated me for allergies, sinus, cold/flu, low iron, and PCOS (poylcysticovarian syndrome). I purchased Apostle John Eckhardt's book, *"Prayers that Rout Out Demons"* and each time I opened it, it opened to the section on witchcraft. I was not familiar with witchcraft at the time so I just closed the book without reading it. Then, one Wednesday night, while I was lying in bed barely able to move, I received a phone call from a minister from our previous church. She said, "Sister Chara, I need to pray with you." As she prayed in the spirit the Holy Spirit began to reveal to her what I was struggling with. She said, "Sister Chara, I see witchcraft and I keep hearing witchcraft." She prayed against the witchcraft that night and reminded me to call on Jesus all the days of my life. The following Sunday at my home church, my Pastor called my husband up to minister to him and while she was ministering to him, the Lord revealed to her what was happening to my body, and she had to fight back the tears. She called me to the front and explained to us that I was under a curse of witchcraft and then the Lord revealed the source. She prayed and broke the curse off my life and then uprooted it from my husband's bloodline. Witchcraft had been a part of his lineage on his maternal side; the Lord instructed her to go back seven generations, which is where it originated. Once the curse was broken off of me and uprooted from my husband's bloodline, I was well in my body. The test that came afterwards was for me to love the person who had been speaking all these things over me.

I come from a long ancestral line of violence, addictions, poverty, incest/perversion, failed marriages, and infirmities on both my maternal and paternal side. The enemy wanted me to believe that I was stuck in these lifestyles. In 2009, I came into the knowledge of generational curses and generational blessings. I learned that is was not meant for me to accept the curses of my ancestors and that God wanted to free me. He wanted me to experience His freedom through His blessings. God will use one person to be a beacon of light for the entire family. Why not allow Him to use you? Choose to live in freedom, allow Him to set you free from the curse of your ancestors. I was one of the individuals in our family that God chose to use. I knew that I did not like living in poverty and I did not have a poverty mindset. When I saw others excelling in life, I knew I could do so as well. I did not covet what others had and I did not live a life of jealousy, but I knew I wanted different and I needed to find out how to get the different I desired. This thirst, to have more than, propelled me to seek God's way even if it did not line up with what family and friends were doing.

GEWWELS, just because you are a member of a family that is filled with alcoholism, drug addicts, sexual abuse, failed marriages, high school dropouts, poverty, sickness, divorce, prostitutes, teenage sex / teen parents, homosexuality, rage, unforgiveness, witchcraft, suicide, depression, oppression, low self-esteem, etc., it does not mean that you will live the same way. God has a plan for your life and His plan is a plan of hope for a successful and prosperous future. One of the things we must do is begin to see the greatness that is attached to our lineage and not focus on the negative. One day in bible study the Teacher said, "see the generational blessings in your family history and allow that to be your declaration." This spoke volumes to me and changed my perspective. I began to reflect on the fact that my family is filled with walking miracles. I was not supposed to be born because my mom was told she could not have any more children. Her and my daddy waited 21 years for my arrival therefore I am a miracle.

Whenever discouragement attempts to distort my day, I remember that I'm a miracle and whatever I'm going through is an opportunity to turn into a miracle. I have a great nephew who was born at 24 weeks old and they never expected him to live through the night, or week, or month, or even year. Now after several surgeries, being told he would not walk, would not talk, and would have brain damage, our little angel is almost five years old, walking, saying words and participating in school like everyone else. He's another family miracle. Then, my own body was in a situation that revealed to doctors that I would be unable to conceive a child on my own. After, two failed attempts of allowing science to help me conceive, God brought forth our very own miracle. I began to focus on what I knew God could do and stopped focusing on what I'd seen with my natural eye. Yes, I experienced the works of evil in my family, but I believed it did not have to be my story and its not. The truth is that I have battled with almost each of the evil works I described above.

However, with a clear understanding that God had different plans for me, I realized that these behaviors were from the enemy, and having a love for God and His Word, propelled me to seek help and get free. You can too. Don't settle for the path that seems to be before you, choose the path that God has for you. You cannot choose your family or lineage, but it is your choice rather to stay defeated or rise to a place where you shine. Maybe your lineage is filled with people who were great with their hands, who owned businesses (tailors, farmers, etc.), or who were great educators, learn of them and press to let that legacy live on, not the negative attributes that are more prevalent. Be determined to be the one who will not let the bad outweigh the good, be determined to be the one who will make a change.

Be determined to leave a legacy that you children

can proudly carry on. Be determined to shift into your shine and not sifted into defeat. Your ancestral line is part of your GEWWELS process that gets you to the place where you shine in purpose. God put you in your family for His purpose, don't deny the people or the process, endure it, learn from it, and let it shape you so you can shine in purpose.

For a long time, I thought I had to fight for everything. Every time someone or something made me mad, I was ready to "throw some hands". In 2009, I learned that God called me to be a prayer warrior. I had to stop fighting in the physical and begin fighting in the spirit. This was a hard transition for me and I found myself doing a lot of crying during this pruning period. Many characteristics displayed in our behavior must be shaped into attributes that can be used for Kingdom building. This hard fact took root in my life when a woman at church was blatantly disrespecting me and attempting to seduce my husband right in my face. I kept trying to tell him about and the leaders but no one would listen. So I began to talk to God about it and I honestly told the Lord I was going to fight her in the church.

One Sunday as she proceeded to bend down in

front of him for the fifth time in 10 minutes, I went to lift my leg to kick her over on the floor to help her get whatever she needed help getting, the Lord would not allow my leg to move and I had to submit to doing it His way. I began to intercede and cry out for her but it was more than what I expected. The Lord showed me why He wanted me to pray for her, because she was not only after my husband, she was after the leadership. I learned about the Jezebel spirit, the Absalom spirit, the Judas spirit, and he Delilah spirit, and how God wanted to use me as a vessel against these spirits of destruction.

The lesson is that we must stop being so easily offended and we must learn that everything is not always about us. Some things are presented to us to birth out a gifting in our life. God knew He created me with the authority and power that comes with fighting. Because this was not cultivated in me as a child as something to be used for God's glory, I used it the world's way. Our personality traits and character are to be used for God's glory, and according to His Word. You should ask yourself what comes natural to you, what disturbs you the most, what causes you to quickly become angry or frustrated? Many of the answers are related to or linked to your family lineage but should be cultivated and used for Kingdom purposes. They are not to be traps to cause you to fall, but beautiful stones that cause you to shine – that radiate His glory in your life.

Chapter 3 – Friendships and Social Relationships

The journey of doing things God's way will seem lonely at times, but once we have an understanding that God is always with us, it is more than manageable, it is peaceful. I remember feeling down once because it seemed as though when I started doing things God's way, my friends began to diminish. One day I said to God, "God, I don't fit in." He replied, "I know daughter, that's because you stand out." He continued, "I did not create you to fit in, I created you to stand out so you can shine in Me, shine in Purpose." He then instructed me to change my perspective.

For the longest time, I found myself going along with the crowd just to say I had a friend. In the end, most of them were not actually friends, they were part of the journey I chose and God used them to thrust me into His purpose. Church was a part of my life from the age of 11, before then, I cannot really recall hanging with many people. As I entered junior high school, I did meet a friend whom I love to this day. She and I did everything together, we dressed alike, wore the same hair styles, we were like family. I was like another sister to her sisters and brothers and like a daughter to her parents. When you saw her you saw me. My mom and sisters treated her the same way. Our mothers even became friends for a time. I learned a lot from her and her family. The great part about our friendship is that she was in church also. My first time experiencing a prophetic word from a man of God was at a service I attended with her and her family. The man of God called me out of the audience to minister to me and I was blown away because I wanted to know how did he know all that he knew about me. It was being in church service with her that I learned about the gift of speaking in tongues and interpretation. Her family opened me up to a whole new life in God and I am forever grateful for her and her family's warm embrace. We went to middle school and high school together, and we graduated together. We even worked our first jobs together. She would tell me when I was wrong and I appreciated her for that. She would tell me what the Bible said about certain things and hold me accountable. Then, in the midst of our friendship, I met another friend who had more of an ungodly influence on my life and I began to hang with her more. That path led me on a quick downhill spiral. I was torn because I knew I needed to hang more with the righteous friend, but I chose to do more with the worldly friend. I wanted to be friends with both so I introduced them to one another and the three of us became amigos. In this friendship, our innocence (in every area) ultimately became tarnished. The truth is that no matter what happened in the relationship between the first friend and me, we always remained friends even if there were a distance in how long we talked or hung out. I must admit that the older I got the more I did to compromise the friendship and I had to repent and ask her to forgive me. She always forgave me and I am blessed for her friendship. No, it's not the same today, but if she needs me or I need her, we know how to reach one another. Overall, I learned that we are blessed with great people in our lives and we should value such relationships. A great friend is one who allows you to be yourself but who wants to see the best of you, so she/he will hold you accountable for doing what is right. They are not afraid to tell you when you are off the mark. They are not afraid to push you in the right direction. Don't be too quick to follow what appears fun and easy. Don't allow yourself to fall into the trap of following those who always pump and prime you, or those who allow you to do things that will hurt you.

I remember after high school, I was with a "friend" and her family on a trip in the Ozarks. We were partying and drinking. We were playing cards and the loser had to take a shot. This night, I kept losing, so I had to take a lot of shots and I was totally intoxicated. I could barely see, but I could hear and the Lord allowed me to hear what I needed to hear to know that these people were not really my friends; they did not really have my best interest at heart. The mother of the group said, "that's on her stupid a** I don't care, she can drink until she pass out." I will never forget it. I woke up the next morning and I knew I would not be visiting them again. It was during this time that I learned about my gift to discern other people thoughts and conversations. My car was leaking oil and I didn't think I was going to make it back to St. Louis, which was two hours away. When we stopped to fill up, my car began to smoke and the friend who was riding with me, she said she needed to ride with her mom, and she left me in my smoking oil leaking car and they sped down the highway leaving me stranded. I learned to really pray that day and I prayed and asked God to get me home safe and He did. I went to their house to get my coat that was there and I knew when I walked out the door that would be the last time I stepped foot in their home. I still had not gotten enough because at the time, I struggled with being alone. I wanted to be with people, I wanted friends; I did not want to be lonely. So I succumbed to being used and abused. I had a car (even if it was leaking) and she did not, so when she needed to go somewhere I was always there because I was out with my "friend." When God is ready to divide and conquer He will do just that. There was another party going on and she needed a ride to the party. When I arrived to pick her up, she looked at me and said, "is that what you are wearing?" I was comfortable with what I had on and the truth is the party was inside someone's home so I didn't see the need to put on anything too fancy. At the party, she left me with people I did not know, and I was totally uncomfortable. Finally, I was with the group where she was and I felt different. She left out for a little while and during her time away I made the decision I was going to leave, but I wasn't sure how to tell her. When she returned to the room, she said, "Um...I have a ride home tonight." I said "OK", I gathered my purse and coat and I left. As I was walking to my car, I heard everything she was saying about me and when I got in my car, I said, "OK God, that's it, I'm done." Yes, I cried because it hurt, but I was stuck in a place spiritually and naturally that was not healthy for me. I was so caught up in wanting a friend on the earth that I neglected to embrace the friend I had in Jesus. I spent so much time with this friend that I had no time for Jesus. When some thing or someone takes all our focus off of Jesus, He will remove it. He is a jealous God and will have no others before Him. Once I was rid of this "friendship" I stopped drinking, stopped clubbing, and began to relax in what was natural to me, which was attending church. I'm grateful for every friendship or social relationship I have had because I have learned a lot along the way and each experience has contributed to my GEWWELS process. The point is there will be many relationships that we encounter and each one of them will contribute to our shaping whether it is positive or negative. We must identify the relationship for what it is – is it good for you or is it influencing you in the wrong direction?

Even relationships that are God-ordained will be tested. Once I totally sold out for Christ, there was a woman in my childhood church who took me under her wings and mentored me. She was awesome. I remember sitting in the back of the church on Sunday when someone tapped me on my shoulder. I looked up and it was her, she said, "come with me, you will not sit in the back of the church any longer." She sat me with her in the front of the church on third pew, right behind the mothers' board. She was very instrumental in my spiritual progression. She had me on a check-in schedule. I had to call every morning before work and every evening after work. I had to attend every Bible class and Sunday School. If I did not have transportation to church, her or her husband would pick me up. If I was low on gas, they assisted me. Even when I moved into my own apartment, I still had to check in. She told me when I moved on my own, "There will be no shacking and no man can spend a night." She meant every word. She kept her cell phone next to her head so if I needed to call at night she would not miss my call. She introduced me to travel outside the United States and cruising. Furthermore, she gave me my first opportunity to speak before a congregation at a 100 Women in White program. I loved her dearly and will never forget how much she did for me. The closer we became the more the enemy began to try our relationship. While working on a program together, we bumped heads on ideas and that was the demise of our relationship. The program turned out great but our relationship suffered tremendously. The day before the program as I left the church to go home, the Holy Spirit allowed me to hear the words she spoke against me and by the time I reached the corner of the church, I was in tears. When I got home, I received two phone calls from other members who wanted to tell me what happened but I would not succumb to the gossip. I told them what was said and they were floored at how I already knew. One lady said, "I just wanted to call and pray with you because what I just witnessed was not right." I told her it was OK, I already knew. I was crushed because I loved her with all my heart and it hurt to know that someone I trusted so much would turn around and spread all my business to other church members. I later learned that it wasn't the first time and that many knew all my business for a long time. I do believe God put her in my life to help me, but I also believe that the enemy was taking what was meant for good and turned it into evil. I never mentioned to her all that I knew, I only continued to love her, but I did step back from all the frequent visits and calls. I slowly accepted that this part of my life was complete. The truth is if none of this would have manifested, I would still be in the same place spiritually, and God wanted me to grow more. I appreciated all I learned and value her input even today. Nevertheless, I learned that relationships will be tested for authenticity. Are you true to God or have you made your truth in this person? Anything that comes before God is an idol and we are commanded to have no other god before Him. Sometimes our friends become our gods, our parents, our jobs, our money, our desire for money, our pastors/leaders, our children, and ourselves. Whatever is before Him has to come down. I was going to her for absolutely everything, she had become my idol, my god and that was not pleasing to God. Be careful in your friendships that you are loyal to them, but that your main loyalty is to God. As a GEWWEL, you cannot shine without Him, but you can shine without certain people.

Chapter 4 – Men and Relationships

Let me begin this short chapter by saying I was a complete mess when it came to men. After the molestations, I became sexually active rather young and quickly promiscuity and perversion entered my life and had its way. Yes, I admit, I participated in many ungodly acts to please men and to get them to like me. This included the acts of group and oral sex. I thought it was the only way to prove that I liked them and it was what I needed to do to get them to like me. Have you noticed that all I wanted was for them to LIKE me? I did none of this with the anticipation of anyone loving me. I found myself in the same situation that I was with females who I called friends; I just wanted to be liked and accepted. Rejection ran deep inside me and I thought if I did what they wanted they would stay. It took me a very long time to understand that all they were doing was using me and what I was searching for could not be found in men. What I needed had to come from God.

Like many females, my mom constantly told me not to have sex before marriage, but I just figured she was old and didn't want me to have any fun. Additionally, I thought how could she tell me this when there was a man living with us and they were not married. They'd lock themselves in the bedroom for hours and leave us in the living room to watch television, how could she not expect us to be curious. I wanted to do what she was doing. From this, I learned that I must live the life I wanted my children to emulate. I couldn't say one thing and practice another. Even if you find yourself in a situation where your parents are telling you one thing and living a different way, be the wise one and do what is correct, not what looks good or what seems to feel good. God has given us these awesome five senses of seeing, touching, smelling, hearing, and tasting. We should always make sure to use them for His glory. He calls us to depend on Him not our senses. Eve got into trouble because of her senses. The Bible says, "When the woman saw that the fruit of the tree was good for food and pleasing to the eye, and also desirable for gaining wisdom, she took some and ate it" (Genesis 3:6). She was deceived because of her senses. Many times we are deceived because of our senses. We see something we like, we hear some words we like, or we feel good and we allow these senses to guide us and often times we are misguided into destruction.

I learned the hard way about not being led by the senses. You don't have to travel that route. Even if it seems lonely for a while, rest in the fact that God knows the plans He has for you and when He releases your husband the relationship will glorify Him. It may not seem like it now, but waiting is worth it. I didn't wait on God and I experienced being raped after a date where the man held a knife to my side and demanded me to "strip or die." Further, I found myself involved with a man who didn't mind killing me if he needed to. He sat outside my house with a gun pointed at me when I walked out the front door. He said, "see I could kill you right now and nobody would know anything." I found myself in cars with men who had people looking for them. I found myself in a long relationship with a man of God who was married. He lied to me and told me he was not married. I was involved with him for almost a year before I learned the truth, and by that time I had strong feelings for him. Additionally, I found myself in a relationship with a pastor who had to keep me a secret because he was dating several other women in the Church. This man had me drinking alcohol, having sex, and even convinced me to do threesomes. To make matters worse, this man of God almost took my life when he almost choked me to death. I dated men that didn't love God and those who had confessed a hope in Christ, but none of them were who God created me to be with, therefore, I was in error and I felt the pain of each one of these relationships.

In addition, I found myself struggling with my sexuality for a time. I knew that the thoughts I was having was wrong but I was so frustrated with going through with men, I thought it would be easier on the other side. Oddly enough, I was not crazy enough to go all the way to the other side, I only played around with it and I felt convicted each time. One Wednesday night at Bible study, I went to one of the mothers of the church and told her what I was doing and what thoughts I was having and she took me in the back mothers' room and took the blessed oil and anointed my body from head to ankle. Then, she told me she was going on a fast for me. I didn't know about fasting at this point but I appreciated her help and support. About a month later, she pulled me to the side and said, "Baby, how is that situation?" I didn't know what she was talking about, and she said, "you know about the girls?" I said, "Ah, I guess it's gone, because I haven't had a thought or act in about a month." This mother sacrificed for my deliverance and my freedom. I received the deliverance and did not have to look back. I learned that there are some people who genuinely care and there are some strong pillars in the house of God that will walk you through your deliverance. I confessed the wrong and God was faithful to cleanse me from all unrighteousness. Your situation may not be as dramatic as mine was, but God wants to heal you and free you from all manners of fornication and perversion. He wants you whole in your mind, body, and spirit. He wants to use your temple for His glory.

Lastly, I remember when God set me free from all promiscuity and fornication. I had made plans to go on a date after Bible Study. As the pastor began the lesson, he said, "I don't know whom this is for, but I hear God say you like to do everything in the dark so that I (the pastor) cannot see you, but I don't have a heaven or hell to put you in. God sees everything you do and your best bet is to live to please Him not me." I was convicted right there in that pew. I never made it on that date that night. When I got in my car, I did an open confession and repented and I went home. I am not sure what God save me from that night, but what I do know is that He saved me. He may have saved me from HIV/AIDS, drug addiction, rape, or death, but whatever trap the enemy had set for me, I'm grateful that God blocked it. It was during this time, I got the revelation of my favorite scripture, Romans 6:23, "For the wages of sin is death but the gift of God is eternal life in Christ Jesus" (NKJV).

I learned that although sin may not take you off the earth immediately, the consequences of sin will and can result in death. It can be a spiritual death, a financial death, an emotional death, or an actual physical death; the fact is there is death waiting on the other side of sin waiting to destroy you. Let's just say you don't get an STD from fornication but you end up pregnant. Ok, so pregnancy is not too bad, its something we can get through, right? Yet what happens when you are stuck raising the child alone, with no extra finances or support, can't finish school or go to college, stuck depending on the government system to tell you when you can shop and enjoy life. Moreover, you can't enjoy life or get a free moment to yourself because you have a child who now depends on you for absolutely everything and you are obligated to care for him/her. No you did not experience a physical death, but emotionally and mentally you are drained, crying and confused. This is what the writer means about the consequences of sin. It may not make sense when you read all the rules about life and sex, but trust God, He put them in place to help and protect you, not hurt you. God loves you and only wants the best for you. He does not want to see his daughters crying or hurt.

Trust His plan when you cannot see His hand. The time will come for you to enjoy the benefits of marriage. However, until you are married, there are no benefits of sexual intimacy. It may "feel" good for the moment, but what are you left with once the moment is over? Men come our way during our GEWWELS journey, but don't be distracted because of how he looks, what he says, or how you feel; wait on God. If you have already indulged in the acts of fornication, forgive yourself, ask God to forgive you, commit to living God's way and prepare to teach the younger generation the lesson of waiting. When your husband is revealed to you, you will know it, but don't go seeking for him, wait on God! Shine in purpose by living according to God word before he arrives and you both can shine in purpose together as God gets glory from His ordained union.

GEWWELS in your pursuit of holiness you will find that our culture exerts tremendous pressure to throw away all moral biblical standards in relationships, but the Bible is clear that one must refuse and abstain from any sexual involvement before marriage. Additionally, one must avoid situations and activities that might arouse or awaken sexual desire before marriage. Be wise, especially when dating. God created sex to be wonderfully fulfilling, but that is only within the secure relationship of marriage between a male and female. You should keep yourself sexually pure for your wedding day.

Your virginity is a gift you can only give once. If it is too late, just ask God to forgive you, purify you, and redeem what has been lost. God is faithful and just to forgive you and He will restore you!

Chapter 5 – Church Hurt

A trick from the enemy! Jesus came that we have life and have it more abundantly. When we are not experiencing abundance in our life we must recognize there is an enemy at work, not God.

If the enemy can distract us with hurtful situations and cause us to focus on people or situations, then he has done his job of taking our focus off Christ. The Bible instructs us to lift our eyes to the hills from whence cometh our help (Psalm 121); further it encourages us to set our affections on the things above (Colossians 3:2). Paul urges us in Romans to live according to the Spirit and not the flesh. Once we make the determination to not be moved by our fleshly desires we will quickly overcome worldly hurt whenever we experience it. The enemy's goal is to get us away from Christ and what better way to do it than by implementing hurt in the one place we are to find comfort, peace, and motivation – the church. This is our first mistake – we put high expectations in imperfect people. Every person in the church organization is imperfect, including the leaders. While we think the local church should be our place of refuge when we are going through difficult times, it is not. That's a hard truth. Nowhere in the Bible is it written that the church building or the leaders or congregation is our place of refuge. However, Scripture tells us several times that God is our refuge, strong tower, hiding, place, or dwelling place. If we can stop running to the people and run to God we will put a halt to the clinging grip of church hurt.

Many times we run to the people because we are looking for someone to feel sorry for us, we are looking for a quick fix. Sometimes it's manipulation – we want something and think the only way to get it is by singing our sad stories to others, thinking it will make them feel sorry and offer some help. That is the quickest way to set yourself up for hurt. Sometimes we genuinely desire help but seek it out from the wrong person. Everyone is not destined to help you. If you must get help, seek the Lord and ask Him to show you who to go to and confide in. It's not always the pastor.

Many leaders are not maliciously planning to hurt

you, it could be that the leader is trying to find you some help and in his/her attempt, lines got crossed and confusion entered. The enemy is going to and fro all day seeking whom he can devour and he will use anyone that allows him. We have to stop operating in our emotions and know what the word of God says. Stand on the principle of what the enemy meant for bad, God uses for your good. We must let go of our pity parties and start praising God in the midst of adversity – knowing that all things work together for good for those who love God and are the called according to His purpose.

I remember my first round with church hurt. I was newly saved at the tender age of 12 years old. I enjoyed going to church, and I met many friends – female and male. Additionally, I felt like I finally fit in somewhere. I was part of the youth choir and participated in all the children activities. Since I was cute and got along with the boys very well, I quickly gained a reputation of being "fast" and "hot." As well, it didn't take long to gain female enemies since we seemed to have interest in the same boys (yes in church). Quickly, things went from bad to worse, as parents got involved and then leadership. I recall my mother being away on a trip and we had choir rehearsal. There was a big commotion and tension was high. After an awkward choir rehearsal, the pastor called me in the office to talk to me. I was the only child without a parent present. As you can imagine, they ripped into me verbally. The children, the adults, and even the pastor; they let me have it. I was told I thought I was cute, I was fast, and they didn't have these type problems until I joined the church. At 12 years old, I was crushed; I was so hurt, I cried profusely. I will say that my mother took care of it after I talked to her, but the cuts had already been made – I was hurt!

I stayed at the church because my mother insisted I stay or else. Things were not the same and I only served the Lord at that point out of obligation or duty and not from the heart. When doing something out of obligation, over time it becomes very easy to stop all together. This is why our conversion to Christ must be done from the heart not from the flesh. It must be done with full understanding of what you are stepping into not based on emotions; it must be done by the prompting from the pulling of Jesus on your heart, not by fluffy flattering words from man. The decision to serve Christ must not be done based on what friends are doing either, it must be a genuine decision to believe that Jesus is Lord and Savior who died and rose from the dead to give you a chance at eternal life. The bottom line is that no matter how awesome a person is there is chance this fleshly person will/can do something that displeases you! But if you give your life to Jesus for Jesus because of Jesus you won't be easily led astray when people fail you.

Once I had the chance to reflect on what actually happened during this adolescent church hurt episode, I came to the realization that even without knowing it, I brought these things on myself. No, it does not give people the right to hurt you but sometimes we must be more careful with how we represent ourselves. I had made a reputation with people by my own actions. Every time they saw me I was in some boy's face, I had the phone numbers of all the boys in the church (probably because of our church phone directory) and the boys responded to me – including the older teens. Therefore, I couldn't be too angry with anyone except myself for allowing the enemy to use me. I wonder how many times we have put ourselves in the line of fire at church and then when the fire actually causes 2nd and 3rd degree burns, then we want to retreat and recover quickly. Some hurt takes longer to heal than others, but the fact is most do heal and they only leave a small scar to remind us to share our story. Many times we are quick to leave the church after we feel we have been hurt after we have brought it on ourselves by our actions. Leaving the church does not fix situation, it does not stop the pain, and it opens the door for more confusion. I find that we have gotten so accustomed to using pain as a scapegoat that we have brought it into the church. When we are in pain, we call off work, we don't go to school, we leave relationships, and now we use pain to opt out of going to church.

Instead of doing what is needed to correct the issue, we run. Leaving the church is not the answer (in most cases); some pain arises so we can get some things on the inside of us worked out. My husband, Bishop Ronald Taylor, says, "God uses pain as a microphone to a deaf world." He insists that God can use pain to get our attention. Pain can cause us to grow and mature if we allow it. Pain can be the beginning of healing and deliverance in areas that are hindering us from reaching our destiny. Don't fight the process; let pain have its perfect way. When you find yourself facing hurt in church, ask God to show you the areas in your life He is trying to prune, or the areas He is trying to shape for His glory. Seek for the positive instead of the negative and watch how God can mend your brokenness and show you areas that He never meant to be in your life in the first place.

The situation I faced as an adolescent brought on some valuable lessons in my life. The enemy wanted to tear down my self-esteem, my identity, and my self-image. He wanted me to walk around in shame with my head held down. If he could achieve this then I would not be effective in my Kingdom Purpose. What better way to do it than by using the person I looked up to the most and as a father figure – the pastor to say, "You think you are cute." To a 12-year-old girl that says *you are not cute.* What girl 12, 21, or 201 wants to be told she is not cute? And the enemy knew that would destroy my self-image especially when there were other underlying issues that already caused insecurity. For me, it was living in poverty in a single parent home with a drug addicted stepdad who had already expressed he didn't like me and a mom who expressed she didn't like me either because I reminded her of my father who had caused her much pain. Since rejection was living in my home, I felt accepted in the church, and then rejection showed up at church and put me back in a place of abandonment. One thing on top of another, the enemy was building his case to take me away from Christ. It was not so much that he wanted me away from church. His purpose is to get us away from Christ.

If we are truthful, many are strong enough to just find another church to attend, so the enemy aims at removing our hope in Christ. There is not another Christ to go to; so he builds all this hurt in the churches so we can give up on Christ completely, but he uses the people and situations in the church. He usually either implements his diabolical plans when we first join as baby saints, or once we have become heavily involved. Either way, most times it's a trick from the enemy. There are times when hurt arrives on the scene at church to get you to move from a place of complacency into a place of destiny. Some of us will not move on our own, so the Lord will allow you to experience the hurt to thrust you into where He has called you in the first place. I experienced this type of hurt at the same church but it was immediately after my wedding. If the pastor had not failed to announce my marriage to the church, I would have never been angry enough to finally leave. Once I finally left the church and got into the place He wanted to grow me then gifts were activated and I was finally able to accept that God had plans for me and it was more than just sitting in the pew. We must determine if the hurt is meant to shape us for destiny or shift us into destiny. One fact is true, hurt is not meant to sift us from God.

During one situation, one of the leaders of the church made inappropriate advances at me. It terrified me so much I had to call the police to my house. I had to go stay with friends because I was afraid. When I brought this to the pastor's attention, he sided with his leader and accused me of welcoming it or initiating it (remember at age 12 I'd made a bad name for myself). I was so hurt and I wanted to leave the church, but God would not allow me to leave. Instead, He made me stay and mature. During this maturation period, I sat in every service with my eyes closed so I could hear the message and not the messenger. I learned how to not get caught up on man, position, flattery, or gifts. I learned to hear the

Word of God. I learned that people are errant but God's Word is inerrant and He wanted me to trust in His Word not in His servant.

Honestly, I did leave the church once more before the final time. I left at the age of 14 after an altercation that led to fighting and threatening of my life. I only visited to support my baby sister when she sang or praise danced. Finally, at the age of 18, during one visit to the church, I felt the Lord tugging me to return to Him and that is what I did. I returned to Jesus, I trusted that He would put me in the church He wanted me to attend. It wasn't until I realized that it was not God who hurt me, it was people. Since God had not hurt me, why was I punishing Him by staying away from the place He wanted to meet me and mature me..

When we leave the church most often we stop praying, stop studying, stop fellowshipping, stop praising, stop worshipping, stop believing, and we definitely stop tithing. If the enemy can stop us from doing these disciplines that keep us connected then he has accomplished his goal. But the good news is he never wins and God will leave a whole flock to come get one who has strayed away. The promises are in

God, not in people. The blessings are from God, not from the people. I urge you do not punish God for what people do.

Chapter 6 – A New Beginning

All jewels (GEWWELS) go through a long arduous process before being ready to shine in purpose. Life's obstacles are part of the process. What you experience in childhood, from your family history, friendships, relationships, church hurt and even in your health are chisels that shape you for the glory of God. In the book of John, there was a man who was blind from birth and the disciples asked Jesus, who sinned the man or his parents? Jesus responded, "Neither this man or his parents sinned, but this has happened that the works of God be made manifest through him" (John 9). You may ask yourself why have all these things happened to you. Rest assured that you experience these things for the glory of God, that God can use you to manifest His love, His power, and His miracles and draw other to Him.

I am not denying the pain that comes along with the process. The pain is designed to bring you to life not make you lifeless. All the painful process to build you up and make you the person you were originally created to be. I admonish you to count it all joy when you experience life's struggles, knowing that the testing of your faith brings patience and brings you into a new place in Christ. The struggles bring you to a place of faith and wholehearted trust and devotion to God. Allow the struggles to nurture your relationship with Christ and bond you so close to the Lord that others long for what you have.

Allow the struggles to break off old habits and strong holds that want to keep you defeated. Allow the struggles to cultivate spiritual disciplines of devotion, worship, prayer, and fasting. Allow the struggles to birth your spiritual gifts. Allow the struggles to bring out your natural gifts and talents. Allow the struggles to shape you into the jewel you were created to be. Walk in full confidence that you are a Girl Entering Womanhood While Experiencing Life's Struggles and this journey will not separate you from the love of God. Be fully persuaded to live a life that is sold out for Christ, not one to please the flesh or the things of the world. Allow the struggles to teach you how to learn His promises and trust His plan. Allow life to happen but only accept that you are called to live life in abundance. You are a jewel! Isaiah 62:3 says, "You shall be a crown of beauty in the hand of the Lord, and a royal diadem in the hand of your God." All He sees is your beauty and He promises that your later will be greater than your former.

The healing that you are now able to receive is preparing you to enter into your new beginning with God. You must know that He is not mad at you for the past mistakes and past sins. Jesus died so you don't have to bear the burden of those sins. Now it is time to go forth and be the GEWWELS He has created you to be. Walk in freedom, impact the world and shine in purpose. People look at you and wonder how you made it through, they wonder why you are not dead, and they wonder why you don't look like what you have been through. It's because you are fearfully and wonderfully made! You are GEWWELS – Girls Entering Womanhood While Experiencing Life's Struggles. Live with integrity! Shine in purpose, on purpose, for His purpose.

Some scriptures for you to reflect on:

Jeremiah 1:5 "Before I formed you in the womb, I knew you; before you were born I sanctified you; I ordained you a prophet to the nations"

Jeremiah 29:11 "For I know the thoughts I think toward you, says the Lord, thoughts of peace and not of evil, to give you a further and a hope"

Romans 8:28 "And we know that all things work together for good to those who love God, to those who are the called according to His purpose"

Psalm 84:11 "No good thing will He withhold from those who walk uprightly"

Psalm 138:8 "The Lord will perfect that which concerns me"

John 10:10 "The thief does not come except to steal, and to kill, and to destroy. I have come that you may have life and that you may have it more abundantly"

Luke 10:19 "Behold, I give you the authority to trample on serpents and scorpions and over all the power of the enemy, and nothing shall by any means hurt you"

Deuteronomy 31:6 "Be strong and of good courage, do not fear nor be afraid to them; for the Lord your God, He is the One who goes with you. He will never leave you nor forsake you"

Psalm 119:133 "Direct my steps by Your Word and let no iniquity have dominion over me"

Psalm 122:7 "Peace be within your walls, prosperity within your palaces"

Psalm 34:17 "The righteous cry out and the Lord hears and delivers then out of all their troubles"

Isaiah 54:17 "No weapon formed against me shall prosper"

Psalm 34:19 "Many are the afflictions of the righteous, but the Lord delivers him out of them all"

Romans 8:37-39 "Yet in all these things we are more than conquerors through Him who loved us. Fro I am persuaded that neither death nor life, nor angels nor principalities, nor powers, nor things present nor things to come nor height or depth, nor any other created thing shall be able to separate us from the love of God which is in Christ Jesus our Lord"

Philippians 3:12-14 "Not that I have already attained or am already perfected; but I press on, that I may lay hold of that for which Christ Jesus has also laid hold of me. Brethren, I do not count myself to have apprehended; but one thing I do, forgetting those things which are behind and reaching forward to those things which are ahead, I press toward the goal for the prize of the upward call of God in Christ Jesus"

Philippians 4:13 "I can do all things through Christ which strengthens me"

Philippians 4:19 "And my God shall supply all your need according to His riches in glory by Christ Jesus" Song of Songs (or Song of Solomon) 8:4 "I charge you, O daughters of Jerusalem, do not stir up nor awaken love until it pleases"

1 Peter 1: 14-15 "But as obedient children, not conforming yourselves to the former lusts, as in your ignorance; but as He who called you is holy, you also be holy in all your conduct."

Notes:

1. www. http://gia4cs.gia.edu/EN-US/diamond-cut.htm

About the Author

Pastor and Overseer Chara A. Taylor is a River of Joy. She began her ministry for the Lord in February 2006, as she launched out in the deep with the mentoring ministry of GEWWELS Inc. (Girls Entering Womanhood While Experiencing Life's Struggles), a ministry encouraging young women to trust God and pursue holiness as they journey through life's struggles transitioning from adolescence to womanhood as the Bible tells us to be holy in all manner of conduct (1 Peter 1:15). It's a ministry of self-awareness and holiness to girls ages 12 - 21. Her mission is to inspire females to understand their individual purpose in Christ, propelling them to shine in that purpose, not being overcome by evil but by overcoming life's obstacles while still living holy.

Pastor Chara truly believes that we are fearfully and wonderfully made to do the will of the Father uniquely as He created us all differently - therefore she encourages young people to learn their gifts and operate / SHINE in that gift/gifts. Her motto scripture is Romans 8:28 "for all things work together for good to those who love God and are the called according to His purpose." Pastor Chara receives great joy from seeing people and businesses go forth in what God has purposed for them.

Pastor Chara carries a smile that brightens up the room and heals people in their desolate places. She is outgoing, bold, and not afraid to go to war with the enemy. Pastor Chara is an effective teacher, preacher, and intercessor for Jesus Christ. She has served as Master of Ceremony for several events and services. She has ministered at 100 Women in White services. She has led various workshops to young women. She hosts an annual Shine in Purpose Conference for young women in St. Louis MO and an annual Mother Daughter Banquet for mothers and daughters to connect and reconnect. She received a Bachelors of Science degree in Christian Ministry in May 2014 from St. Louis Christian College, where she graduated top of the class as Valedictorian and was inducted in the Honor Societies of The Association of Biblical Higher Learning, Stone-Campbell Journal Honors, and Sigma Lambda Chi-Chi, with the help of God.

In July 2014, Chara was elevated to Overseer by her spiritual parents and covering Apostles Robbie and Sharon Peters of Kingdom Empowerment International Covenant of Fellowship Churches, Inc. She loves family and having fun!

One of her greatest testimonies is the miracle birth of Isaac Jeremiah Taylor, her baby boy! After being told she would not conceive - God miraculously gave her the child she longed and prayed for 5 years. In this, she learned how to keep the faith in God, continue to do His work, trust His timing...She learned that waiting on Lord does pay off. She has launched Hannah's Cry prayer call to inspire other married women and couples who are waiting and believing God for a child. She launched Bible Babies Inc., a retail store of biblically inspired clothing for babies. Further, along with her husband Bishop-Designate Ronald, she assists inspiring couples to live godly marriages according to Ephesians 5. Their One-Flesh Ministry is called Ephesians 5 Husbands and

Wives. Overseer aspires to do things Gods' way, which is why she believes in living Holy, in fear and reverence of the Lord always. Overseer believes if you live biblical principles, you will receive biblical promises!

www.ingramcontent.com/pod-product-compliance
Lightning Source LLC
LaVergne TN
LVHW051135080426
835510LV00018B/2423